DO SING

RECLAIM YOUR VOICE.
FIND YOUR SINGING TRIBE.

JAMES SILLS

Published by
The Do Book Company 2019
Works in Progress Publishing Ltd
thedobook.co

Text © James Sills 2019
Illustration © Hannah Cousins 2019
Photography
p67 © Sarah Bush 2019
p109 © Paul Marbrook 2019
p112 © Tory Williams 2019

To find out more about our company,
books and authors, please visit
thedobook.co or follow us **@dobookco**

5% of our proceeds from the sale of
this book is given to The Do Lectures
to help it achieve its aim of making
positive change **thedolectures.com**

Cover designed by James Victore
Book designed and set by Ratiotype

Printed and bound by OZGraf Print
on Munken, an FSC-certified paper

A CIP catalogue record for this book
is available from the British Library

ISBN 978-1-907974-70-0

10 9 8 7 6 5 4 3 2 1

CONTENTS

PROLOGUE

Manchester, September 2002

He stood on the top of the grand piano with a huge grin on his face. And each time he lifted his arms, two thousand people lifted their voices, creating a rising wave of harmony that swept across the room. He closed his eyes then raised his arms one more time, seemingly reaching for the heavens. The combined voices of the crowd sustained a final glorious chord — we wanted to stay in that moment forever — and then it was all over.

The choirmaster that evening was songwriter Ben Folds. We had entered the venue to watch him in concert but, partway through, the traditional audience / performer relationship changed. We had been turned into an impromptu backing choir by the irrepressible Ben, being taught to sing in perfect three-part harmony. Leaving the venue with my friends that night, I knew we had shared something very special. To be part of that sound felt utterly consuming, exciting, extraordinary. However, it was the ordinariness of the experience that also struck me. We were just a regular crowd, in a regular venue, on a regular Thursday night. Yet we had created something beautiful, memorable, life-affirming.*

* The song was 'Not the Same' by Ben Folds. You can hear a version of this, complete with audience choir, on his album *Ben Folds Live*, released in 2002.

INTRODUCTION

I believe in the power of singing. Like laughing and dancing, it is a simple and joyful expression of our humanity that is best when shared with other people. There is something intrinsically good about singing with other people, on a musical and human level. To sing in a group is an act of love, for yourself and for other people. I know because my own life has been transformed by singing.

These days, I am the guy at the front, leading groups of people in harmony singing, trying to create something extraordinary from the ordinary. Currently, I run several weekly choirs and while each group is very different, the benefits experienced by their members are the same. And this is what I want to emphasise in this book. Whoever you are and whatever stage of life you're at, singing has the capacity to be life-enhancing and, in some cases, life-saving.

This book is for everyone, as everyone has the capacity to sing. It is one of the great human universals. But if it's for anyone in particular, it is for those people who may have stopped singing, or who think that singing is not for

them, or who might be thinking of joining a choir for the first time. I hope that this book will inform, encourage and inspire you to go out into the world and sing with others.

Do Sing is divided into three parts:

Part One will help you reflect on the role of singing in your life and highlight what prevents people from accessing group singing (spoiler alert: mainly themselves!) I will also tell you a bit more about my own singing journey and put forward my ideas about everyday singing.

Part Two is all about the benefits of singing with other people, drawing on my own experience, scientific evidence and through powerful testimonies from members of my various choirs.

Part Three aims to give you the information and confidence to reclaim your voice and find your singing tribe.

My motivation for writing this book is to pass this on, to share the love. At its core, *Do Sing* is about how singing can be a vehicle to us leading better, healthier and more fulfilling lives. And, as the great Ella Fitzgerald said, 'The only thing better than singing is more singing.' So, let's get started.

PART ONE

WHAT'S YOUR SONG?

**Let us go singing as far as we go:
the road will be less tedious.**

Virgil

CHAPTER ONE
EVERYDAY SINGING

Humans have always sung. In fact, there is evidence that singing developed before spoken language. There is no known human culture that does not sing. Some anthropologists believe that because singing in a group is a sociable, inclusive and co-operative activity, it provided an evolutionary advantage for early humans. The Greek philosophers also understood this. Plato asserted, 'All well-bred men should have mastered the art of singing and dancing.' In the sixteenth century, English composer William Byrd argued that 'the exercise of singing is delightful to nature, and good to preserve the health of man'.

However, in the modern world, many people have become estranged from singing. People tend to view themselves as either a 'singer' or 'non-singer'. And there seems to be a lot more in the 'non-singer' category. Most people who come to my choirs or workshops tell me that they haven't sung since their school days. And in Chapter 2, we'll look at why that might be.

THE SONGS WE SING DEFINE WHO WE ARE (AND WHO WE WANT TO BE)

Songs are powerful. They help define who we are as individuals and in our communities: they also define certain periods of our lives. Musician and psychologist Daniel Levitin identifies six different functions that a song can fulfil:

1. **Friendship**
2. **Joy**
3. **Comfort**
4. **Religion**
5. **Knowledge**
6. **Love**

— Daniel Levitin, *The World in Six Songs*

Songs become the soundtrack to our lives and help us to understand the world around us. But most of us have become used to being passive receivers of such songs, rather than active participants. We might sing along in the privacy of the shower or the car, but feel inhibited to do the same with other people. Therefore, we tend to only sing at those big moments in life where we feel obliged — weddings, funerals, celebrations. But group singing is something we can access all of the time, and it can enhance our everyday life. To misquote a phrase: singing is for life, not just for Christmas. So, what's stopping us? We'll look at this in more detail in the next chapter, but for many people the term 'choir' is the first barrier.

WHAT IS A CHOIR?

I've recently started a monthly singing session in my local pub. It's called the 'Glynne Arms Pub Choir'. We meet on the last Sunday of each month and I teach two well-known songs in two-part harmony. It's fun and friendly — people feel relaxed in a more informal environment and quickly lose their inhibitions when singing as part of a big group. But is this really a choir?

The definition of 'choir', according to the *Cambridge Dictionary*, is 'a group of people who sing together'. So yes, the Glynne Arms Pub Choir certainly fits the description. And I will use the term 'choir' throughout this book to mean singing groups.

However, 'choir' can be a loaded word. It might make you think of formal groups, reading from musical notation, performing in churches or concert halls. Or it might make you think about contemporary choirs popularised through film and TV, such as *Pitch Perfect* and *Glee*. For many people, these provide short cuts to what singing in a choir is about.

But there is a whole world of singing beyond the churches, concert halls and the glee clubs. It is for this reason that I consciously avoid describing myself as a 'choirmaster' and prefer 'vocal leader', which feels broader and more inclusive. Likewise, I don't always include the word 'choir' in the names of the singing groups I lead. My caution in using the word 'choir' isn't a value judgement, but part of my way of making singing more accessible.

WHAT IS EVERYDAY SINGING?

To make singing more open and less scary we need to start thinking about it in a different way. We need a model that is more inclusive and normalises group singing as part of everyday life. I call this *everyday singing*, which is also the name of my blog.

The four principles of everyday singing are:

1. The belief that singing is something that we can all access without the need for special training.

2. That it takes place in visible, everyday places/spaces such as community centres, workplaces, hospitals, schools, cafes.

3. That singing experiences are integrated into the fabric of social/work life such as community choirs, workplace choirs, singing groups, workshops, festivals.

4. An emphasis on the process, rather than the product — the holistic aspects of the experience are more important than a final performance.

In this book, I'm here to tell you that singing is for you. It's for *everyone*. And you can do it *anywhere*. Singing together isn't the preserve of a particular culture or musical tradition. Or a particular place.

Here are some places that I've led singing over the last ten years:

— Around campfires   — Do Lectures
— Football stadiums   — Hospital wards
— Pubs   — Workplaces
— Churches and cathedrals — Schools
— Music festivals   — Libraries
— Homeless shelters   — Community centres
— In the streets

What do these places have in common? They are simply places where people gather. And where people gather, people can (and should) sing.

It has been heartening to see the rise of organised everyday singing in recent years, in the form of community choirs, workplace choirs, 'sing for health' choirs and choirs driven by a social purpose (such as choirs for refugees, homeless people, military wives, etc.) Also, I encourage you to check out the work of Pub Choir (Australia), Koolulam (Israel) and Choir! Choir! Choir! (Canada), all of whom organise huge, joyous, one-off singing events around the world. Participants come together for a few hours, learn their parts and then perform, which is filmed and put online.

It is my hope that everyday singing will continue to move further into mainstream consciousness, so that singing will be thought of in the same way as everyday exercise or everyday healthy eating. In fact, I can find many parallels between the realms of group singing and running.

WHY SINGING IS LIKE RUNNING

Singing, like running, is part of our collective history as a human species — it's part of our DNA. Singing and running are immersive experiences that significantly contribute to individual wellbeing. We can access them both freely — we already have the equipment. However, until a few years ago, I was very much of the opinion that running wasn't for me (just as people think that singing isn't for them). Like many non-singers, it stemmed from a childhood experience in which I was ridiculed in public by an authority figure. In my case, it was my PE teacher telling me, 'My toddler can waddle faster than you can run.' I believed him and didn't consider running again for another two decades.

I used to think that running was about technical perfection and competition, as many people think about singing. But as I tentatively worked my way through the couch-to-5K programme to my first Parkrun, then from 10K races to running half-marathons, I started to realise that, for me at least, running is basically about creating headspace and feeling good, both physically and mentally. And I've now found a lovely running group where I live in North Wales that enjoys the experience of running together without feeling the need to compete and compare times. Sure, there is a focus on technique and self-improvement, but not at the expense of the bigger picture. And it feels great to have a support network.

The most important thing is the *doing* and not thinking too much about it. With running, it's simply putting on your kit and heading out of the door. With singing, it's about opening your mouth and allowing yourself to become immersed in the sound. But if it's that simple, why do we sometimes stop singing?

If I cannot fly, let me sing.

Stephen Sondheim

I want to sing like the birds sing,
not worrying about who hears
or what they think.

Rumi

CHAPTER TWO
WHY WE STOP SINGING

Despite everything we've said so far about its importance, the reality is that many people do stop singing. For many, the idea of singing in public is associated with thoughts of anxiety, judgement, fear, embarrassment. Sounds familiar? I get it. I've met a lot of people who feel like this. And I want to tell you that it's perfectly normal. There are a lot of (incorrect) deeply held beliefs and myths that lead us to believe that singing is something that someone else should do. But here I'd like to dispel those myths and show how singing really is for everyone. It's time to reclaim your voice.

I'M TONE DEAF – I CAN'T SING

Do you enjoy listening to music? If so, then you are not tone deaf. The technical name for this clinical condition, *amusia*, affects approximately 4 per cent of the population and those with the condition are unable to process and replicate musical sounds. Therefore, if you derive pleasure from listening to music, you are indeed capable of singing. Linked to this is a belief that singing is something you simply can or can't do. In my days as a school teacher, I explained to my pupils that singing is like any other skill. You start simply, you go from A to B to C. Don't run before you can walk. There are simple steps you can take to do with your breath, body and voice that will help you prepare for singing — some of these can be found in Part Three.

I WAS TOLD THAT I HAVE A BAD VOICE AND SHOULDN'T SING

This is possibly the most common reason that people give to me for stopping singing. And it's the one that runs the deepest, just like my experience with the PE teacher at school. This humiliation, often by an authority figure, typically happens in school years and can be very damaging indeed. I heard a story once about a public school that divided pupils up into categories of bird according to their singing 'ability', with nightingales at one end of the scale and crows at the other. I think there might have been badges. I'm wincing just at the thought of this. Because the voice is one of the most personal things we have, it is part of our identity. It is the instrument that we all carry with us, all of the time. And so when our voice is criticised then we feel personally criticised. But for many people, this is a watershed moment in their singing life. They believe what they are told. And let me tell you, you can sing.

I'M WORRIED WHAT PEOPLE MIGHT THINK IF THEY HEAR MY VOICE

The great thing about singing in a group is that you become part of the bigger whole, which means that your voice will only be heard as part of the choir rather than as an individual. And the bigger the choir, the more you will be supported by the other voices. So many of my choir members say something along the lines of, 'I think I've got a terrible voice, but together we sound great.' And this is the beauty of group singing. Sure, there are some choirs that might give opportunities for soloists should they wish, particularly in classical and musical theatre styles, but in a choir the emphasis is on the communal, not the individual.

I HAVEN'T HAD ONE-TO-ONE SINGING LESSONS

Don't tell anyone, but neither have I! (Well, only a handful) I'm very much of the opinion that being in a choir is the perfect way to develop confidence and a musical ear as a novice singer. You are supported by other voices and won't be put 'on the spot'. You learn to listen and blend. Most choirs will start a rehearsal with warm-ups, which are essentially ways of exploring and awakening yourself to the possibilities of your own voice. Some of these vocal exercises are listed in Part Three and would be a good starting point if you've stopped singing. However, if you are experiencing vocal health problems or are interested in solo singing, I would recommend finding a singing teacher for some individual lessons.* But generally speaking, I don't think these are necessary to engage in group singing.

I CAN'T READ MUSIC NOTATION

While many singing groups, particularly more formal or classical-based choirs, use musical notation, the majority

*A good book for vocal technique is *This is a Voice* by Jeremy Fisher and Gillyanne Kayes

of singing global cultures do not. Musical notation is a much more recent development than singing. The sound is the important thing. Think back to that time you sang nursery rhymes as a child. Or were in the crowd watching your favourite band. None of these experiences required musical notation. There are many choirs that teach by ear, which means listening and copying back. Some will distribute lyrics sheets and make learning materials available online, which is what I do with my choirs.

I WANT TO SOUND LIKE MY FAVOURITE SINGER [INSERT NAME HERE] BUT I DON'T

Firstly, unless you're a very experienced impersonator, it's highly unlikely your voice will sound anything like your favourite singer, or anybody else for that matter. Why? Basic physiology. As vocal expert Ian Davidson explains, 'Not everybody has the same shaped head, same neck-length or 101 variables that can contribute to making up a person's sound.' Secondly, there is the broader question of why you would want to sound like someone else. Your voice is as unique as your fingerprints and these differences should be celebrated. Imagine if the likes of Bjork, Thom Yorke, Tom Waits, Aretha Franklin, Joni Mitchell and so on had spent their careers trying to sound like someone else. What I love about those singers is that you can't mistake them for anyone else — their voices are unique.

To an extent, it is also a matter of genre. For example, if you want to sing musical theatre or opera, there are certain 'blueprints' of those styles you'll need to adopt in your singing. But always keep 'you' in there too.

Finally, it may be damaging to try and emulate another singer. I know many vocal coaches who refuse to teach songs by 'belters' to young singers whose vocal physiology hasn't fully developed.

I'M TOO SHY TO JOIN A CHOIR

If *Pitch Perfect* and *Glee* are held up as the standard, you might think that to be in a choir you have to be all-singing, all-dancing, all-jazz-hands. Those among us who identify as introverts may find the thought of being part of this awful and completely overbearing (for the same reasons that those with more extroverted tendencies might find this appealing). Firstly, not all choirs are like this. For example, I know many groups that are devoted to gentle, meditative singing and chanting. But whatever the genre of music, singing in a choir is always a collective experience, where the individual can be subsumed into the whole. This can provide a safe, secure and supportive environment for people who might think of themselves as naturally introverted. A good choir director should help you grow in confidence as a singer. Indeed, in my experience it can often be more difficult for extroverts to blend into the choir dynamic.

I DON'T HAVE THE TIME

There are many different ways to engage in group singing, and not all of them involve a lengthy weekly evening rehearsal. For example, workplace choirs are becoming more and more commonplace, many of which take place at lunchtimes or at the end of the working day. I have run workplace choirs in both timeslots. One of the first choirs I led was a staff-and-student school choir, which rehearsed for thirty minutes once a week during lunchtime. One of the regular members was a deputy head, who described choir as her 'weekly therapy session'. Despite having a huge number of responsibilities, she resisted the temptation to work through her break and engaged in singing, knowing what the benefits would be. Other alternatives to weekly rehearsals include one-off workshops, monthly singalongs and residential singing holidays. Some of these will be discussed in Parts Two and Three. There is also the fact that, to an extent, we all choose to prioritise how we spend our time. If you spent less time on social media and television, chances are that you would free up extra time for reading, exercise ... or joining a choir!

IT'S TOO EXPENSIVE

If you're not able or ready to commit financially to a choir — payments are usually termly, but many have weekly or monthly options — you could always do what composer and producer Brian Eno did and start your own singing group at home with friends. 'A few years ago, a friend and I realised that we both loved singing but didn't do much of it. So we started a weekly a cappella group with just four members. After a year we started inviting other people to join. Well, here's what we do in an evening: we get some drinks, some snacks, some sheets of lyrics and a strict starting time. We warm up a bit first.' Like I've said, you already have the equipment you need, and singing can take place anywhere.

I DON'T KNOW WHERE TO START LOOKING FOR A CHOIR

Easy — read Part Three of this book!

CASE STUDY

Cath is a team leader in an NHS hospital and mum to two children. She didn't sing in a choir until a few years ago, due to pressures of work and family life plus not 'having the courage to just go along and have a go. Also, it seemed that choirs were too far away from where I lived and I knew nobody.'

Now, however, singing is really important to her: 'Life is so busy and so hard sometimes, but singing is my release. When I am feeling stressed and I know I have choir practice coming up I know that for that hour or so my stresses disappear. The choir has been a great strength to me, it is uplifting. I recently lost a loved one and to come to choir has really, really helped my wellbeing.'

Cath's example shows that if we are able to work through the things that are preventing us from singing there are great rewards to reap.

Life is a song — sing it.

Shirdi Sai Baba

CHAPTER THREE
MY (SLIGHTLY UNORTHODOX) SINGING JOURNEY

Before I ask you to reflect on your own relationship with singing, I thought I'd tell you a bit more about my journey that led to me becoming a full-time vocal leader and singer. It's a slightly unorthodox journey. It started three decades ago, not at a choir rehearsal, but on a Saturday afternoon at a football stadium. So, here we go, in (nearly) ten steps:

ONE

My earliest memory of being immersed in joyful and whole-hearted singing was on the football terraces with my dad. I was five and it felt so completely exhilarating to be one among thousands of voices, cheering on our team Coventry City FC and singing:

> *Let's all sing together, play up Sky Blues,*
> *While we sing together, we will never lose,*
> *Tottenham or Chelsea, United or anyone,*
> *They shan't defeat us, we'll fight till the game is won.*

Football was my first passion until my late teenage years, when music took over. Although my interest has waned as I've become older, it was a huge honour for me to lead a choir singing 'You'll Never Walk Alone' on the pitch at Anfield, home of Liverpool FC, several years ago.

TWO

Singing was certainly part of my childhood, though it definitely wasn't centre stage. I sang in assembly at school, at the church in my village and at the football. I knew I could hold a tune but certainly didn't consider myself to be 'a singer'. In hindsight I can see that this was a very healthy attitude: singing was part of my everyday life and was something I simply *did*, either with classmates, friends or family. It was simply part of being in those communities.

THREE

One of my earliest musical loves was the band Queen. I remember watching a documentary about the band in which guitarist Brian May said, 'Being in the crowd at a rock concert is an amazing feeling — it's like being at a football match, but everyone is on the same side.' As I entered my teenage years, I came to recognise and immerse myself in this feeling. And it's something that still thrills me. Recently, I saw Paul Simon and James Taylor perform at London's Hyde Park. It was brilliant to see two of my favourite songwriters on the same bill, but the magic really happened when fifty thousand people joined together to form an impromptu choir to sing such timeless songs as 'Homeward Bound' and 'Fire and Rain'.

FOUR

I've always been more excited about group music-making than performing solo. I didn't take singing lessons at school, but had weekly tuition in piano and trombone. Despite my teachers and parents' encouragement (and patience), I wasn't disciplined enough to spend hours rehearsing in a room on my own. But when I was making music with others, whether it be in the school jazz band, orchestra or brass group, I found my place, both musically and socially. This is brilliantly summarised here by conductor Gustavo Dudamel, which can equally apply to singing in a choir: 'My education was sitting in an orchestra. And what a beautiful model for a society. Everyone together, listening to each other, with one goal. This is the best way I can think of to build a better world.'

FIVE

My teenage years were soundtracked by 'Britpop' bands such as Oasis, Blur, Pulp and a number of other British bands. It was an exciting time for British guitar music and popular culture in general. Accordingly, I taught myself a few chords on the guitar and learned some of my favourite songs. It wasn't long before I was asked to join a band covering the likes of Nirvana and Green Day. In some ways, these three or so years of playing, writing and gigging with my best mates were the most formative. Being in a band is to be part of a tribe. And it was at this point, I knew that music would be my path through life.

SIX

During my university years, I developed a deep interest in music psychology and considered further training as a music therapist. Having a sister with cerebral palsy makes me acutely aware of the positive impact music can have on people with disabilities. To this day, we still love to go to concerts and sing together — ABBA's 'Dancing Queen' is our karaoke classic — and I'm delighted that she's recently joined a local choir. So, from an early age I've been aware of how music can be a positive, life-changing force.

SEVEN

After university, I started to lead singing for the first time as part of my work as a freelance music educator, despite regarding myself as a non-singer. My first choir was at an inner-city primary school in Liverpool where I ran the after-school choir. We'd sing positive, affirmative songs such as 'Lean On Me' and 'I Can See Clearly Now' and I loved the energy that emanated from rehearsals. Interestingly, most of the attendees were boys, skipping football practice to come and sing (as you'll read in Part Two, a big part of my current work is encouraging men to sing).

EIGHT

The way I now think about singing was very much informed by a year spent living in Ghana, West Africa, in my mid-twenties. Here, I was teaching music while also learning and performing with local musicians. Music and especially singing was very much part of the fabric of everyday life and it was at this time that I started to realise the *why* of group singing: for your voice to be heard and to express yourself as part of a community. It wasn't about the individual or 'getting it right' but simply *doing*. Since then, my guiding principle of singing has been this Zimbabwean proverb: 'If you can walk, you can dance, if you can talk, you can sing.'

NINE

For most of my late twenties and early thirties, I worked as a classroom music teacher in a secondary school. Singing was part of this, everything from running choirs, to school productions, to mentoring solo performances. But only a part of it. Outside of teaching, I set up my first community choir and began to deliver singing workshops at weekends. I also began performing more and more with the Spooky Men — an all-male choir — both in the UK and in Europe. It reached a point where the thing I loved doing the most — the singing — had to fit into the limited time and energy I had after a week of teaching. I remember returning to work after a long summer of singing and someone saying, 'Back to reality now.' But I knew that the reality I wanted was one where joyful, community-based singing was centre stage. Within a month I had handed in my notice, and here I am, a few years later, writing this book for you.

There was nothing inevitable about my path as a vocal leader. Indeed, I am not a formally trained singer and I haven't grown up in a formal singing world (you may think I'm not qualified to write this book!) But looking back, I believe I had the right attitude to singing because I didn't really *think* about it too much. I didn't have the same hang-ups as when I took my instrumental music exams. I didn't put any pressure on myself. Put simply, singing has always been part of my life — and increasingly so. I encourage you to make singing part of *your* life, if it isn't already.

———

SO, WHAT'S YOUR SINGING SOUNDTRACK?

Try these three exercises:

1. **Imagine what the showreel of your life might look like so far.** Not just the highlights but the stuff that really means something, the big and small. The things that really mattered and continue to matter to you. What would the five defining moments be? Take a moment to decide before moving on to the next exercise.

2. **Now, think about the music to accompany your showreel.** Not an epic sweeping film soundtrack with soaring violins and trumpet fanfares, but the music, songs and lyrics that are meaningful to you. Again, choose the five most important pieces. Take yourself back to the time you either first heard these pieces of music or to a specific 'peak' moment when you found yourself lost in the music. Remember how it felt.

3. **Finally, consider the role of singing in your showreel.** What five singing moments would you include?

You've already read about my singing journey, or soundtrack as I like to call it. Here's a few other prompts to help you reflect on yours:

— Your childhood: what songs do you remember singing at home, in the car, at school, at celebrations, or family events?

— Do you remember singing as part of a crowd at gigs or festivals? Did you play in a band or sing in a choir?

— What about the ceremonies that mark the beginning and end of life: baptisms and funerals?

— Perhaps there have been other moments, such as singing around a campfire or at a big sporting event where you felt the power of being at one with a big group.

— Is there a song that you and a friend or partner consider to be 'your song'? And can you think back to when you sang it together?

— If you have children in your life, what songs did or do you sing with them?

I suspect that out of the three exercises, it is the last one that will evoke the strongest memories, perhaps some uncomfortably so. Singing is hardwired into our souls and songs accompany the peak moments of our life. Indeed, awareness of sound is one of the first senses to develop in the womb and one of last faculties to go at the end of our lives. Songs are literally with us from the cradle to the grave.

When you get blue and you've
lost all your dreams,
There's nothing like a campfire
and a can of beans

Tom Waits, 'Lucky Day'

CHAPTER FOUR
GATHER ROUND

When was the last time you sang around a fire? Maybe it was part of a camping trip, at a festival, at summer camp or a night on the beach? These are modern incarnations of something much more ancient, as old as humanity itself.

We have always gathered around fires to sing and tell stories. And traditional rituals involving singing are practised around the world to this day. For example, it is still an important part of ancient rites in Shaman culture. Songs are sung around the fire to connect individuals with the spirit world. Singing is also seen as part of the healing process and maintaining inner balance:

> In many shamanic societies, if you came to a medicine person complaining of being disheartened, dispirited, or depressed, they would ask one of four questions: 'When did you stop dancing? When did you stop singing? When did you stop being enchanted by stories? When did you stop being comforted by the sweet territory of silence?'
> — Angeles Arrien, foreword to Gabrielle Roth's *Maps to Ecstasy*

There is something very elemental about sitting around a fire with other people. It gives us a chance to stop, take stock and enjoy the present moment. And as the night deepens and the embers glow, we take comfort in the warmth of the fire and start to relax in the company of others. The world becomes a little softer and gentler for a while. And it gives us an opportunity to slow down and remind ourselves of the simpler pleasures of life, whether it be conversation, stargazing, storytelling, cooking, dancing or singing.

As I reflected on my own experiences of group singing as I wrote this book, some of the most vivid and precious memories have been those around a fire. Here are five of them:

1. **Covean beach, St Agnes, Isles of Scilly, UK, every summer from 2002 to 2008**
   WITH: fire spinning, wild swimming, dancing
   MOST MEMORABLE SONG: 'Dreaming Of You' by The Coral

2. **Lake Bosumtwi, Ghana, 2007**
   WITH: djembe, beers, dancing
   MOST MEMORABLE SONG: 'One Love' by Bob Marley

3. **National Youth Music Camp, Wavendon, UK, 2008**
   WITH: cocoa, blankets, lanterns
   MOST MEMORABLE SONG: 'Viva La Vida' by Coldplay

4. **Creative Mornings Summit, New York, USA, 2018**
   WITH: s'mores (toasted marshmallows held in a biscuit sandwich to the uninitiated), moonlight, dancing
   MOST MEMORABLE SONG: 'Faith' by George Michael

5. **Do Lectures Farm, West Wales, UK, 2018**
   WITH: bread baked in the fire's embers, whisky, dancing
   MOST MEMORABLE SONG: 'All Night Long' by Lionel Richie

My happiest day would be to find a meadow, light a fire and cook a big meal. I'd play my guitar or just listen to bird song. Music, food and good company is, as far as I'm concerned, the elixir of a good life.

— Cerys Matthews

IS SINGING TOGETHER HYGGE?

Singing around a fire is undoubtedly a very human and connecting experience. It allows us to wonder at the universe and reconnect with ourselves and each other in very fundamental way. There is also something about the physical cosiness that is akin to the Danish concept of *hygge*. This is explained by Meik Wiking, from the Happiness Research Institute in Copenhagen:

> Hygge is about an atmosphere and an experience, rather than about things. It's about being with the people we love. A feeling of home. A feeling that we are safe, that we are shielded from the world and allow ourselves to let our guard down.
>
> — from *The Little Book of Hygge*

According to this definition, I would definitely describe singing around a campfire with others as *hygge*. But is this describing the singing or simply the feeling of being with others? I asked my friend Bodil, who sings in the a cappella choir Vokalkompagniet in Copenhagen, whether or not she considered singing to be *hygge*. She said, 'Singing to me is a happy place where I forget all about my job, my obligations, my frustrations, my worries, my self-awareness. It's one of the only situations where I'm actually able to be present in the moment. But then the *hygge* part comes afterwards. When we go to the pub for a beer and a chat about the small and big things in life. THAT'S *hygge* to me!'

CLASSIC CAMPFIRE SONGS

After years of playing guitar around different campfires, on three different continents, there are some classic songs that seem to just work, songs that transcend time and place. Here's a few suggestions to get you going (it's not just 'Kumbaya' or 'Ging Gang Goolie'!) Songs that work well around the fire are those that have lots of repetition for people to join in and are positive and celebratory. Why not add a few of your own?

— **'House of the Rising Sun'** by The Animals

— **'Stand By Me'** by Ben E. King

— **'Twist and Shout'** by The Beatles

— **'Big Yellow Taxi'** by Joni Mitchell

— **'Can't Help Falling in Love'** by Elvis Presley

— **'Hallelujah'** by Leonard Cohen

— **'Wonderwall'** by Oasis

— **'Brown Eyed Girl'** by Van Morrison

— **'Talking 'bout a Revolution'** by Tracy Chapman

— **'Three Little Birds'** by Bob Marley

— **'You've Got a Friend'** by Carole King

MY SINGING MANIFESTO

I believe that singing around a fire provides us with the perfect model for inclusive, joyous and meaningful group singing. I would like to put forward my own singing manifesto based on this, which can apply to all group-singing contexts. These, I believe, are your rights as a singer. And in order to experience the full benefits of singing, the following should be true of the group with whom you are gathered, whether it's a bunch of mates in your front room or a choir of a thousand people.

1. You should be welcomed and feel part of a community

2. You should be valued and 'seen'

3. You should be supported and not judged

4. You can be completely in the present moment

5. You can connect with your breath and body in a positive way

6. You can connect with and express your emotions in a positive way

7. You can sing!

PART TWO

WHY WE NEED
TO KEEP SINGING

**Live in the present,
launch yourself on every wave,
find eternity in each moment.**

Henry David Thoreau

CHAPTER FIVE
CONNECT

The most immediate benefit of singing is connection. Singing in a group connects us to ourselves, to our emotions, to other people and to the present moment. It is the latter that I will focus on in this chapter. Because if we're not fully present when we're singing, we won't begin to experience the other benefits. Is your phone off? Let's go ...

THE AGE OF DISTRACTION

We are living in the age of distraction. An ever-increasing number of things are vying for our attention, with our smartphones being the biggest culprits (in order to get this chapter written I had to turn off the Wi-Fi and my devices as well). We allow ourselves to be interrupted by texts, email and social-media notifications. This makes it difficult and sometimes impossible for us to feel fully present. Even when our devices are hidden away, the maelstrom of everyday life — balancing our commitments to work, friends, family, finances — can make for a very busy mind indeed. The result can be a feeling of disconnection.

'NO-PHONE' RULE

There is growing recognition that phones are a barrier to meaningful engagement with the present moment. While they can help us connect with the rest of the world, they often lead to disconnection in face-to-face gatherings. Priya Parker addresses this in her excellent book *The Art of Gathering*: 'The reality [is] that people are often elsewhere, thanks to their technological devices. Perpetual distraction is a curse of modern life and of all modern convening in particular. And when we do come together, our minds are in a thousand places.'

In order to try and remedy this problem, you might adopt a 'no-phone' policy during shared meals with friends. In recent years, we've seen the rise of 'no-phone' gigs, where audience members leave their phone in the lobby and are not allowed to bring it into the main auditorium. This is to encourage the audience to engage more fully with each other and with the music. Musician Jack White has been a big advocate of no-phone gigs and recommends that you 'enjoy looking up from your gadgets for a little while and experience music and our shared love of it in person'. Likewise, many people are choosing to go on distraction-free holidays, either where phones are banned, such as on retreats or meditation residentials, or else they head off to a remote area where there is no reception or Wi-Fi. When I tutored at the National Youth Music Camp in the UK, teenagers handed in their phones at the start of the week. After initial withdrawal symptoms, they always found this to be a positive thing. Many described the experience as 'being in a bubble' for the week: completely centred on their music-making and forging new friendships, they could savour the moment and not think about how they would 'frame' their experience for social media.

SINGING US BACK TO THE PRESENT

There are other remedies for the age of distraction, which can help bring us into the present moment, and they fall into two broad categories:

Practices that focus on controlled breathing and physical discipline to encourage mental stillness, such as mindfulness, meditation and yoga (if you want to find out more about this the book, *Do Breathe*, by Michael Townsend Williams is a brilliant place to start).

1. **Immersive activities** such as reading, surfing, cooking, running or crafting, which enable deep engagement in something and allow us to 'get in the zone'.

I would argue singing brings together both of these remedies: it is an immersive activity that requires controlled breathing and physical discipline. Singing helps us reconnect with ourselves and with the present moment in three main ways: breath, focus and submission.

> **The effects of outside stresses in daily life seem to melt away. Knowing this time belongs to me, no distractions, just focusing on learning the songs and enjoying the sound.**
> — Toria, 39, creative agent

BREATH

Singing is an aerobic activity that requires careful and controlled breathing. Many vocal leaders — myself included — will start a rehearsal or workshop with simple breathing exercises. Some of the ones I recommend are in Part Three of this book. The purpose of these exercises is twofold. Firstly, it helps members to slow down, focus and 'arrive' in the room. I have found this to be especially important for workplace choirs, where members often come straight from their desk, hospital ward or wherever, and they need a buffer between the world of work and the world of choir. Secondly, it prepares them more specifically for the demands of singing, which is particularly important when singing long passages where greater breath control is required. Through simple breathing exercises, our blood becomes more oxygenated, meaning that overall alertness is improved. Other benefits include the reduction of stress and anxiety.

MULTIPLE FOCUS

It's fair to say that when you're singing in a group, there's a lot to focus on at any one time. You'll be concentrating on delivering the lyrics, whether you have memorised them or are reading from a lyric sheet. You may also be using musical notation. At the same time, you'll be listening closely to yourself and to the other members of the choir. You'll be listening to the voices in your section within the group to see how this fits in with the bigger picture. You'll be constantly adjusting what you're doing to blend with the group sound. If your group has a leader, you'll need to watch them carefully for further musical directions, such as beginnings, endings, changes in volume, changes in speed. There may also be synchronised movement, whether it's hand claps, stomps or choreographed dance moves. Yes, singing in a group is a multi-sensory experience!

Don't worry if this all sounds scary, though — a lot of this you will do intuitively, and a good musical director will lead you through the rest.

For two hours every Monday night I can't think about work, I can't look at my email, I can't check Twitter, because I am concentrating hard on something that doesn't come easily to me. This is deep work and it's of immeasurable value to my mental health.

— Richard, 43, brand strategist

SUBMISSION

There is also a sense that when you're singing in a group, you are giving part of yourself up to the greater whole. You become part of something bigger, and many singers report a feeling of getting 'lost' in the music.

When you sing with a group of people, you learn to subsume yourself into a group consciousness ... the immersion of the self into the community. That's one of the great feelings — to stop being me for a little while and to become us. That way lies empathy, the great social virtue.

— Brian Eno

Music that has lots of repetition can aid this process. For example, I teach a lot of music from different African traditions, which are typically based upon the repetition and layering of short phrases. Once the phrases have initially been learned, singers report finding real liberation, because they are not having to think about what is coming next and can fully engage with the present moment. Likewise, music for meditation tends to use lots of repetition, which can have a trance-like effect.

Many choirs and vocal groups choose to perform without any musical notation or lyric sheets in their hands (which is the default setting for my choirs, wherever possible). For many people, the notation or lyric sheet becomes another barrier, either between them and the musical director or between them and the audience. It is very easy to 'hide' behind a lyric sheet, both practically and metaphorically. To sing without something in your hand can be unnerving, you feel more exposed. However, it opens up the channel of communication, and allows you to fully submit to that moment. It also provides a good mental workout for individuals, requiring singers to memorise lyrics and music (and possibly dance moves too!)

> **Singing is a break from the work/life stresses. Taking time out to have some fun and relax with like-minded people. It's a focus away from the day-to-day.**
> — Gareth, 49, accountant

Having established a sense of connection on a personal level, we then start to experience connection and synchrony with other people, to which I now turn.

I love to hear a choir. I love the humanity ... to see the faces of real people devoting themselves to a piece of music. I like the teamwork. It makes me feel optimistic about the human race when I see them co-operating like that.

Paul McCartney

When you sing with two or three other people and you get it right — everything lifts a couple of feet off the ground.

Graham Nash

CHAPTER SIX
SYNCHRONISE

It is one of the simplest and most fundamental human pleasures when we synchronise our activities with other people. Whether we're co-ordinating movements, such as clapping or dancing, or co-ordinating our voices when chanting or singing, it feels intuitively good. It gives an immediate sense of community and unity. And it's something that is seen across all of human culture.

THE POWER OF THE HANDCLAP

The most commonly heard song in our household at the moment is the children's song 'If You're Happy and You Know It Clap Your Hands'. My young daughter loves it. When we do the movements together, whether it's clapping hands, stomping feet or reaching for the sky, she is obviously thrilled. She's just over a year old, but already recognises the pleasure of co-ordinating movement with other people.

If you've ever been to a live music performance, whether it be a small venue or a large stadium, you'll know the power of the handclap. Often it is the highpoint of a performance, where the artist wants to unify the crowd or create a 'peak' moment. It's something that I try to incorporate at some point when my choirs perform. The band Queen understood this brilliantly, incorporating handclaps into several of their big songs, such as 'Radio Gaga', 'We Will Rock You' and 'Another One Bites the Dust'. As they were playing to huge stadiums, with hundreds of thousands of people in the audience, the handclap provided a simple but brilliant way of uniting the whole crowd.

In traditional African culture, the most fundamental way to participate in a musical performance is through singing and the handclap. While there will be many layers of complex rhythm being played by highly skilled drummers, there will always be a handclapping pattern that is simple enough for everyone to join in with.

SINGING AND SYNCHRONY

When we're singing together, there are many levels of synchrony. Singing is similar to chanting in that it involves the co-ordination of words and rhythm to a set beat (pulse), which is essentially an extension of speech. But singing it also requires different pitches (the high and the low notes). These different pitches used in a song can determine how difficult it is to sing. Many children's songs, nursery rhymes and folk songs tend to have a smaller range of pitches, which make them easier and more accessible for everybody to sing ('If You're Happy and You Know It', for example, has just seven different notes). More complex songs, often those from opera and musical theatre styles, will have a bigger range of pitches and more tricky rhythms. This means they are more difficult to synchronise in a bigger group. It explains why not all 'classic' songs will necessarily work when sung by a group.

A good musical director will recognise it and should tailor the musical arrangements to the ability of the group.

One of the most powerful examples of synchrony is when we sing in unison, a word which comes from the Latin *unisonus*, meaning 'having one sound, sounding the same'. It simply means when everyone is singing the same thing, i.e. the tune without any harmony, such as when you sing 'Happy Birthday to You' at a friend's party. It's what I experienced in those early days on the football terraces, singing with thousands of people in unison.

As well as words, rhythm and pitch, there are many other musical variables that can be synchronised within a group. These include:

— **Dynamics:** volume

— **Blend:** the way the voices sound as one

— **Timbre:** the tone quality or 'colour' of the sound

For further explanations of musical terms, see the Glossary at the back of the book.

'WORDLESS' SINGING

Another way to achieve synchrony when singing is to do away with words completely and just use vowel sounds. There are examples of this in most singing cultures. Scat singing in jazz, through singers such as Louis Armstrong and Ella Fitzgerald, turned wordless singing into a whole new art form for soloists. Contemporary classical composer Karl Jenkins used this really effectively in his 1994 composition 'Adiemus'. Other examples of wordless singing include the 'fa-la-la' refrains of English madrigals and the

Beatles singing 'nah nah nah, nah-nah-nah-nah, nah-nah-nah-nah' at the end of 'Hey Jude'. The frontman of Queen, Freddie Mercury, frequently used vocal improvisations in live performances for crowds to copy, using meaningless vowel sounds such as 'day-oh' (see footage from their 1985 *Live at Wembley* for a great example of this). Similarly, the band Coldplay also incorporate repeated wordless refrains into their songs. Not only does this create a powerful way for audiences to join in, whether or not they've heard the song before, but it's also a way for people who speak different languages to engage with the songs.

SYNCHRONISING HEARTBEATS

Musical synchronisation is not the only thing that happens when we sing together, however. A study in 2013 found that when we sing together in a group, our heartbeats start to synchronise. Yep, you read that correctly. Our *heartbeats* start to synchronise. This revelation led to widespread press coverage and the following headlines:

> **'Choir singers synchronise their heartbeats'**
> — BBC News

> **'Many hearts, one beat: singing syncs up heartrates'**
> — *TIME* magazine

> **'Choir singers' hearts beat as one'**
> — CNN (blog)

The study, by Dr Bjorn Vickhoff, found that singing, like yoga, was effective in regulating the breathing patterns of participants. And, through a number of exercises in which he monitored the heart rates of singers performing the same songs, he found that their heart rates fell and rose together according to the demands of the song. For example, when singing a long phrase on the outbreath, heart rates fall, whereas when taking an inbreath before a new phrase, heart rates rise. So, the effect of a group singing — and, most importantly, breathing — together is that their heartbeats rise and fall together. As Vickhoff said, 'When you are singing, the heartbeat for the whole group is going up and down simultaneously.' He also recognises the powerful effect this can have on group dynamics: 'One need only think of football stadiums, work songs, hymn singing at school, festival processions, religious choirs or military parades. Research shows that synchronised rates contribute to group solidarity.'

THE JOY OF SYNCHRONY

In a 2009 study at Stanford University, Wiltermuth and Heath found that synchronous activities can help create deep social bonds, even among members of a group who hadn't met previously. Participants in their study felt a greater sense of belonging and inclusion within a group when they were synchronising with other people. Wiltermuth and Heath concluded that this may have evolutionary benefits: 'Synchrony rituals may have therefore endowed some cultural groups with an advantage in societal evolution, leading some groups to survive where others have failed.'

Having looked at the way singing entails multiple layers of synchronisation, we can see that the effect of this is a feeling of solidarity: a key element of group singing. Let's see how this works.

Let's get together and feel alright.

Bob Marley

CHAPTER SEVEN
HARMONISE

When we sing together, we create harmony. Not just musically, but in the broader sense of the word. 'Harmony' comes from the Greek word *harmonia*, which means 'joined, in agreement, concord'. And this is what it feels like to sing together: a feeling of connection, unity and fellowship. To sing together is to be part of a community. Your voice is heard. It's powerful. And there's never been a greater need for this.

AGE OF LONELINESS

Humans are social beings: we all need regular face-to-face contact with others to chat, laugh, sing or just have a coffee. We need to be seen. But we're living in an age where we're seemingly becoming more isolated from each other. There are many complex reasons for this. But what we do know is this: as each local shop, cafe, library, community centre, bus route or factory closes, we lose the potential for interaction with other people. Writer George Monbiot says: 'Communities have been scattered like dust in the wind. At work, at home ... we are atomised.'

He calls this the Age of Loneliness. And loneliness can

affect anyone, anywhere, of any age, of any demographic. Loneliness is considered one of the greatest social concerns of our age, and is having a corrosive effect on mental and physical health. Recent research found loneliness is as damaging to our health as smoking fifteen cigarettes a day. We now have a Minister for Loneliness in the UK. It's clear that what we need to do, more than ever, is foster community wherever we can. Community that is positive, vibrant and inclusive. As the Beatles said, we need to come together, right now.

REKINDLING OF COMMUNITY

The nature of community is changing: we're starting to see new ways for people to connect. Examples on a local level include community-owned shops, local currencies, time banking (a reciprocity-based system in which skills are shared and hours are the currency), co-operatives and volunteer schemes. On a national (and international) level, organisations such as Sunday Assembly, Men in Sheds, University of the Third Age, Creative Mornings and Parkrun are helping to build meaningful community through face-to-face interaction.

HOW THE INTERNET CAN HELP YOU FIND YOUR TRIBE

It would be easy to blame the internet for the decline of traditional community. True, we can now do our shopping, watch films, read books and engage in conversation through our screens. We could all benefit from a digital detox every now and then. But the reality is that the internet is part of our lives. And it can help you find your tribe. The Do Lectures and Creative Mornings have vibrant online communities. And most people join my community choirs after visiting our website. They can find out who we are, what we're about and watch some of our performances. An email or two later, they're coming through the door to sing at their first rehearsal. They can then listen again to rehearsals online and post on our choir Facebook page. Here the online experience facilitates and enhances the real-world community.

WHAT IS IT ABOUT SINGING AND COMMUNITY?

There is something particularly special about singing and the way that it builds and strengthens community. On a musical level, being in a choir requires collaboration and co-operation, working together towards a shared goal. You are encouraged to listen, to blend and to become part of the greater whole. If you have ever felt the thrill of singing in a group (and I hope that you have), you will recognise this feeling.

There are many powerful examples of how singing can be used to bring together individuals and strengthen community ties, particularly at times of hardship, such as song in the civil-rights movement and chain-gang songs for prisoners in working parties. Here, singing together isn't just a way to boost morale but also a way of reinforcing and bonding the group. And while we might have grasped this intuitively, there's a growing body of research that recognises the benefits of singing in a group.

Nick Stewart, a psychologist at the University of Bath, found that those who engaged in group singing reported greater psychological wellbeing than those who were involved with solo singing or team sports. They also felt more fulfilled and motivated. The interesting thing here is that there is a distinction between solo and group singing. To feel the benefits, you need to be singing with other people, not just on your own in the shower!

> **There is a wonderful feeling of exhilaration and euphoria that comes from singing together with other people. It is a very positive and mutually supportive experience. The best kind of teamwork.**
> — Brian, 53, solicitor

Another study by researchers at the University of Oxford found that adults who sing in choirs bond more quickly with other people than those who undertake other activities (such as creative writing, craft, etc.) They referred to this as the 'icebreaker effect'. Their findings showed that while other activities gave more opportunity for talking, singing together gave individuals a shared goal and was therefore a more powerful icebreaker. They concluded:

> In light of mounting concerns around loneliness and isolation and the increasingly urgent search for solutions, it is fascinating that people seem to be returning to an interest in connecting with one another through singing. The evidence indicates that our singing ancestors might have held a key to better social wellbeing.
> — Jacques Launay and Eiluned Pearce

SINGING ON PRESCRIPTION?

In the UK, there is growing recognition within the health
sector that participation in group activities, such as singing,
can have beneficial effects on wellbeing. Social prescribing
(sometimes called community referral) is a process where
doctors, nurses and other primary care professionals
refer patients to a range of local, non-clinical services.
This can include participation in arts activities, sports
groups and volunteering, all with the aim of improving
both physical and mental health. There are calls for
'singing on prescription' from various musical and medical
professionals.

SING WHILE YOU WORK

In the pre-industrial age, singing often accompanied
manual work; we see this in field hollers and sea shanties.
The singing helped synchronise movements while helping
bond the group at the same time. The rise of industry
in the Victorian era saw the growth of male voice choirs
in coal- and tin-mining communities. In a sense, these
were the original community choirs. Their legacy is
still felt today. While the mines and pits are long gone,
there are still many male voice choirs, particularly in the
old mining regions in Yorkshire, Cornwall and across
Wales. But there's also been an explosion of choirs in
the contemporary workplace, rehearsing at lunchtimes
in offices up and down the country. Workplace choirs
were the focus of two recent BBC television series, with
workers from such diverse employers as an airport, a water
company, a fire service and a supermarket.

The benefits for both employer and employee are clear.

Workplace choirs can:

— boost morale and contribute to staff wellbeing

— encourage teamwork across different departments

— help foster new friendships and build community

— make staff feel more positive about their workplace

— create performance opportunities for workplace events

I currently run two workplace choirs, one for staff at a children's hospice and one at an NHS hospital. Members come from all departments such as clinical staff, administration, finance, volunteers, etc. Singing together is not only a powerful leveller, but contributes to a sense of belonging.

> **It's a time where you can forget about work. You might have had a stressful day but you leave choir with a spring in your step. It's so nice to be part of a group: you don't feel individual, you just feel part of one big team.**
> — Ruth, 58, financial manager

BEYOND THE SINGING

Many choirs have a strong emphasis on socialising, ranging from a cup of tea in the break to week-long residential holidays. It is no coincidence that both of my community choirs rehearse within a couple of minutes' walk of the local pub, where conversation and often more singing ensue. Due to the democratic nature of singing, choirs are often multi-generational with people from a wide variety of backgrounds. We have end-of-term feasts, where food is shared and choir members elect to do a 'turn' of music, poetry or comedy. We also raise a huge amount of money for both local and national charities, which gives members a further sense of purpose and pride. Other choirs hold quiz nights, dance evenings, trips to concerts, residential holidays. A choir, in effect, becomes an informal support network, where deep friendships are forged.

> **I've met, and formed lasting friendships with, people from so many different walks of life with so many different perspectives. Evenings in the pub, walks in the countryside, dinner parties, days out, holidays and visits all across the country — all of these can be traced back to choir.**
> — Ian, 30, academic

The need for meaningful community is especially important for those living more at the margins of society. The Choir With No Name (CWNN) is a charity in England that runs choirs for those who have experienced homelessness and other forms of marginalisation. Currently, they run four choirs (London, Brighton, Birmingham and Liverpool) that rehearse weekly and perform regularly. I am lucky to have worked with their Liverpool choir on several occasions and have always come away feeling uplifted and more optimistic about the world. Their spirit and energy is contagious.

CWNN put community building at the heart of what they do; after the rehearsal, all of the choir members and volunteers sit down to eat together. It's a chance to unwind, chat, and to have a good meal. Many members say that this is the highlight of their week. And it's a model that we've adopted at the Welsh sister choir to CWNN that I direct called the Wrexham One Love Choir.

Many members consider their fellow singers as family, as choir member Mark explains.

> I say it's like a family here — and it really does feel like that. People come, do something together, join in and can always talk to someone if they need to. It's like an outlet. The singing helps people to build confidence and allows them to let their problems out. It gives them a group of people they can trust.
>
> — Mark, 45, Wrexham One Love Choir member

In their 2018 survey of CWNN members:

— **96%** said they had made new friendships

— **76%** reported improved mental health

— **93%** have improved in confidence

Therefore, the singing can be seen as a vehicle for members to develop a greater sense of community, confidence and structure in their lives.

> The choir has actually saved my life without them even knowing it, because they helped lift me out of a dark place with their joyful and non-judgemental attitude and amazing friendly atmosphere.
>
> — Gareth, CWNN Liverpool choir member

Through these powerful personal testimonies, backed up by scientific research, we can see that singing plays a significant part in building community. We will now take a closer look at the physical changes that occur in individuals when they sing together.

I believe music is like medicine.
Like a good tonic, it can open your mind,
strengthen and possibly even cure you.
Music can work on many levels,
and nothing I know of possesses the
healing force that exists within music.

Burning Spear

CHAPTER EIGHT
RELEASE

To sing together is to experience release or letting go. The release of the self into the collective. The release from everyday 'busyness' into the stillness of the present moment. And there's increasing recognition that singing together is fantastic for individual wellbeing, due to the emotional, physical and hormonal release experienced when singing with others.

EMOTIONAL

As we saw in Chapter 1, singing is hardwired into us as humans. We have songs for all of the big moments in life: births, deaths, weddings, celebrations. For example, 'Happy Birthday to You' is thought to be the most widely recognised song in the English language. Coming together to sing is a safe and healthy vehicle for us to express ourselves, both individually and collectively.

We South Africans sing before we sleep, when we are happy, we sing when we are sad. It's a healing thing.

— From the film: *We Are Together*, 2006

Singing your heart out when times are good is easy. It's thrilling and intoxicating. It feels like you are floating on air. But less so when times are hard. I frequently have choir members who have a quiet word with me before a rehearsal to let me know of a recent hardship, often the loss of a loved one. Frequently, I observe singers having a tearful moment during a rehearsal or performance. And, for most of the time, I think that this is a positive thing. Singing together is cathartic. It helps us say the things we need to say. And when we do this as part of a group, we feel both comforted and strengthened.

Songs are like poems in that they carry meaning, but the meaning of the words can be heightened in songs by the musical setting. Take the poem 'Crossing the Bar' by Alfred, Lord Tennyson:

Sunset and evening star,
And one clear call for me!
And may there be no moaning of the bar,
When I put out to sea,

But such a tide as moving seems asleep,
Too full for sound and foam,
When that which drew from out the boundless deep
Turns again home.

Twilight and evening bell,
And after that the dark!
And may there be no sadness of farewell,
When I embark;

For tho' from out our bourne of Time and Place
The flood may bear me far,
I hope to see my Pilot face to face
When I have crost the bar.

We sing a musical arrangement of this poem with the Spooky Men's Chorale that is both tender and powerful. It feels cathartic for us singing it on stage, likewise for audience members, who will often approach us after a gig and tell us what this song means for them. And it has a special resonance for me too, as it was played at the funeral of my stepfather. While I've sung this hundreds of times, it continues to move me (if you'd like to hear it, search for 'Crossing The Bar' + 'Spooky Men' + 'Ely Cathedral' on YouTube).

MEN AND SINGING

Part of my mission as a vocal leader is to encourage more men to sing. To sing in a group is to make yourself vulnerable, and we know that, generally speaking, men are not always good at this. I find it shocking and disturbing that the most common form of death for men in the UK under the age of forty is suicide. The many reasons for this are complex, of course, but an overriding factor seems to be the reluctance of men to talk about their feelings. We are told to button up; we are told to 'man up'. We are not encouraged to open up or express ourselves, whether it be through song, prose or visual arts. But we should. And singing in a group provides a healthy outlet where your voice can be heard. For example, Paul, a member of my community choir, says:

> **It's an uplifting and nourishing thing to do — when you've had a tough day or a tougher week. It's cathartic to sing your heart out in a welcoming and friendly environment. I enjoy the sense of pride in what we do as a choir.**
> — Paul, 48, teacher

This applies whether it's singing sea shanties, love songs or comedy songs. In a recent radio documentary on men's singing in the republic of Georgia — which has a long and rich tradition of men singing together — singer Charlotte Church observed, 'Worldwide there's this idea of toxic masculinity. But there's this real bond between men when they sing and emote and express together. And that's really healthy.'

Men's singing groups can provide an alternative to other all-male environments, such as sport and the workplace, which are frequently based on competition and a culture of macho one-upmanship. In contrast to this, to be part of a choir is to listen, collaborate and create together.

PHYSICAL

There are a number of health benefits associated with group singing, which stem from the fact it is a controlled aerobic activity which both relaxes and energises the body.

RELAX

As we saw in Chapter 5, regulated breathing through singing can help lower blood pressure and alleviate symptoms of stress and anxiety. Through paying attention to posture — especially the neck, shoulders and back — engaging in singing can have further physical benefits. Paying attention is key here: we often go through our days without considering our posture, which is to our detriment. Sustained periods of driving or sitting at our desk, for example, can create tension in our neck and shoulders. Stress and anxiety often manifest themselves in this way, too. However, when we are singing, tension is our enemy. It is for this reason that I will always incorporate simple exercises to relax the shoulders and open up the back at the start of rehearsals. Not only does the singing sound better, but the singers feel more present and in control. Some of these exercises can be found in Part Three. They are designed to reduce muscular tension and to be accessible to all. This is especially valuable to older people or those with limited mobility. Margaret, a sprightly 86-year-old member of one of my community choirs, recognises how the physical benefits of singing can be linked to her own health:

> **In physical terms, it requires correct breath control which exercises the throat and reduces body tension. Mentally, this helps create feelings of peace and calm.**
>
> — Margaret, 86, retiree and great-grandmother

ENERGISE

> **I feel uplifted and awake after every choir rehearsal, even if I arrive exhausted and in a bad mood. It feels wonderful.**
>
> — Ian, 30, academic

Through paying attention to your breathing and posture, you are likely to feel more alert and energised, even before you've started to sing. And, like I've said, singing is physical — it's a whole-body experience. So, when movement is incorporated into the singing, the energy level — both individual and collectively — can go off the scale. Just watch a gospel choir in full flow — it is a joyous experience. The energy is palpable.

There are many singing cultures where singing and movement are interrelated, so the separation of the two would be completely artificial. This is the case in many traditional African cultures. For example, South African choir Ladysmith Black Mambazo incorporate synchronised leaps, kicks and arm movements into their singing. Likewise, the style of music popularised by films such as *Pitch Perfect* put a strong emphasis on choreography. In both of these cases, you couldn't imagine the performance without the movement: they are equal parts of the performance.

However, you don't need to dance like a Zulu warrior or Beyoncé to bring movement into your singing. Many of these are genre-specific, but ways that movement can be used in group singing include:

— **handclaps**

— **finger clicks**

— **stomps**

— **moving from side to side on the strong beats** (e.g. beats 1 and 3 in a pattern of four)

— **body percussion**

— **movement around the stage**

— **fully choreographed dance moves**

This then creates a virtuous circle of energy, where the movement enhances the singing, and the singing enhances the movement: they become synonymous.

CHEMICAL RELEASE

There's a lot going on physically when you sing in a group. And this includes the release of hormones associated with mood elevation and reducing symptoms of depression. These are endorphins, dopamine and oxytocin.

Endorphins

Endorphins are chemicals produced naturally in the nervous system that both relieve pain and elevate mood. In fact, the word 'endorphin' comes from *endogenous*, meaning 'of the body', and 'morphine', which is a known pain-reliever. Many studies have highlighted how singing together in a group stimulates the release of endorphins into the brain, such as this one from 2012:

> Singing, dancing and drumming all trigger endorphin release in contexts where merely listening to music and low energy musical activities do not. We conclude that it is the active performance of music that generates the endorphin high, not the music itself.
> — Study by R.I. Dunbar et al

Basically, endorphins are a natural high produced by our bodies. And there are lots of ways that we can boost endorphin levels, such as regular exercise. Anyone who has ever experienced 'runner's high' will know this feeling.

Dopamine

Dopamine is a neuro-transmitter that regulates different functions in the body, including sleep and digestion. It is essentially a 'reward' hormone. The sense of satisfaction that we feel when completing a task is due, in part, to a rush of dopamine. This can be linked to most enjoyable experiences in life, including singing! Whether it's learning a new harmony part, finishing a song in rehearsal, or performing in front of an appreciative audience, singing provides many opportunities for a rush of dopamine.

> **After a song when you get a cheer, or after a show when you get positive comments from the audience such as 'That was beautiful' or 'You guys make a great sound', it's a great kick.**
> — Kevin, 61, clinical researcher

Not only does dopamine positively affect your mood — and therefore can be linked with alleviating depression — but you are more likely to get a good night's sleep!

Oxytocin

Oxytocin is often called the 'love' hormone, as it plays a particularly important role in human-to-human attachment. The release of oxytocin is linked to trust and bonding, feelings that are frequently experienced when singing as part of a group. There is much ongoing research in this field related to singing. These studies are working on the principle that the release of oxytocin may help to explain why groups bond so quickly during singing. This links back to using group singing to combat loneliness and depression for people who feel isolated.

Furthermore, there is also evidence that singing, as well as elevating mood, helps reduce cortisol levels in the blood, thereby helping alleviate feelings of low mood and stress.

WELLBEING

As we have seen over the last few chapters, there is an overwhelming amount of evidence, both from personal testimonies and academic research, that group singing plays a crucial role in individual wellbeing. Singing helps promote social cohesion and encourages good physical and mental health, which may boost mood and help alleviate depression.

5 STEPS TO WELLBEING BY SINGING TOGETHER

According to the NHS, the five steps to wellbeing are: connect, be active, keep learning, give to others, be mindful. All of these can be applied to group singing:

1. **Connect:** singing brings us together as a community and helps forge strong social bonds.

2. **Be active:** singing is an aerobic activity that regulates breathing while also relaxing and energising the body.

3. **Keep learning:** singing uses different parts of the brain as you process new words, melodies, rhythms, etc.

4. **Give to others:** you are giving in a musical sense when people hear you perform; also, most choirs are socially conscious and are active fundraisers.

5. **Be mindful:** singing is a multisensory experience that encourages you to be fully present (mindful) and may result in a state of flow.

We're lost in music; feel so alive.

Sister Sledge

CHAPTER NINE
FLOW

As we have seen, singing in a group has the capacity to be uplifting, comforting, energising and joyful. It may also be conducive to the state of flow. You probably know that feeling: when you are so deeply immersed in something you lose all track of time. Everything else fades away for a while; you are completely 'in the zone'. Many psychologists believe that the flow state is the ultimate condition for human happiness. It's what makes us feel truly alive. And it's something we can experience when singing together. But when was the last time you experienced flow? Last week? Last year? In your childhood? Or are we too busy chasing the wrong things?

Traditional narratives tell us that our personal happiness is linked to status and material gain. And that true happiness is always just around the corner, whether it be in the form of a promotion, a bigger house or new car. However, this is an imperfect system: the nature of our restless human brains is such that once novelty fades, our expectations rise again and we continue in our quest to 'keep up with the Joneses'. So, if it's not the empty promises of capitalism, where can we find true happiness and fulfilment?

THE POWER OF EXPERIENCE

Professor Thomas Gilovoch of Cornell University conducted a 20-year study into happiness and concluded that true happiness comes from experiences and not material possessions. He argued:

> Our experiences are a bigger part of ourselves than our material goods. You can really like your material stuff. You can even think that part of your identity is connected to those things, but nonetheless they remain separate from you. In contrast, your experiences really are part of you. We are the sum total of our experiences.

This is echoed in the work of Bronnie Ware in *The Top Five Regrets of the Dying*, whose conversations with patients in palliative care led her to write about the regrets of those in the last days of their lives. These centred around regretting working too hard and not allowing themselves to experience life fully, such as staying in touch with friends and allowing themselves to be happy.

Unfortunately, in the twenty-first century, the singing experience has become commodified and competitive. We are encouraged to be passive listeners by the recording industry, spending our money to appreciate the talents of those who 'can' sing. And, through certain prime-time TV programmes, singing is turned into a cut-throat competition, where the reward is the promise of a recording contract and a glittering career. There is also the prevalence of 'Battle of the Bands' competitions for young musicians. The implication here is that musical performance is only about competing. This notion of 'getting it right' is reinforced by the importance attached to passing musical grade exams. These can all be summed up as: Too much emphasis on the final product and not enough on the process, the experience of getting there. Which is where the real joy lies.

IT'S ABOUT THE JOURNEY

Singing, and music-making in general, is something that is intrinsically valuable in itself, not just because it might lead to a moment in the spotlight or an impressive exam score. This is something I would always tell my pupils taking public exams: your final grade reflects how good you are at fulfilling the exam board's specification, it doesn't grade your worth as a musician! For this reason, in my choirs and singing workshops, I always emphasise the process over the product. It is the shared experience of listening and working together — learning the parts, building up the harmonies — that is the real thrill. The alchemy of when it comes together for the first time.

> **When the song starts to take shape and the harmonies start layering and you feel like you fit in and contribute to that sound, totally present in that moment — wow!**
> — Toria, 39, creative agent

This isn't to say that I don't have high standards for my groups when they perform. My aim is for my choirs to perform with passion *and* polish (a phrase coined by fellow choir leader Helen Yeomans). I see performances as an outcome of the rehearsal process, rather than the sole purpose for the group existing. It's like running: what really matters is that I enjoy it as part of a routine: getting my trainers on, heading out onto the trails, feeling those endorphins. Doing it week in, week out: making it a habit. Doing a race is fun, but once you start to become obsessed with your time and personal bests, running can become another part of life that is competitive. Before you know it, you're keeping up with the Joneses again (and there's a lot of Joneses in Wales). Whether it's running or singing, the important thing is that what you're doing is enjoyable in itself, rather than simply as a means to something else. As the famous quote goes, 'It's about the journey rather than the destination' (attrib. Ralph Waldo Emerson). And this is one of the conditions for achieving flow: that what you're doing is intrinsically rewarding in itself.

CONDITIONS FOR FLOW

Flow is being completely involved in an activity for its own sake. The ego falls away. Time flies. Every action, movement, and thought follows inevitably from the previous one, like playing jazz.
— Mihaly Csikszentmihalyi

In his 2014 TED talk, the founder of flow theory, Mihaly Csikszentmihalyi, explained that once basic needs have been met, there is little correlation between income and happiness. Therefore, happiness is more likely to derive from experience than from acquiring material possessions. Through interviews with artists, musicians and scientists he found a common state of 'flow', whereby day-to-day reality is temporarily suspended and replaced with a different reality. This can result in a state of ecstasy — from the Greek for 'to step aside' — where you are completely engaged in the present moment. Following thousands more interviews with people from across different cultures, he summarised what it feels like to be in flow. All of these are highly relevant to the experience of group singing:

1. **Completely involved and focused**

2. **Outside of everyday reality** — a sense of ecstasy

3. **Inner clarity** — knowing what needs to be done

4. **Knowing that the activity is achievable** — our skills are adequate

5. **Sense of serenity** — no worries, no ego

6. **Timelessness** — focused on the present

7. **Intrinsic motivation** — the activity is a reward in itself

If we want to achieve the flow state through singing, we have to consider number four carefully. For you to achieve flow, it needs to be challenging and within your current skill set. You want to feel like you are being pushed, but not out of your depth. It's a fine balance. And it's a consideration when choosing songs to perform and when joining an existing choir as a new member — and we'll come to this in Part Three.

PART THREE
TAKE ACTION

THE FIRST STEP

In Norway, there's a word for that feeling of dread when you are about to undertake a new task for the first time — *dørstokkmila*, which translates as 'the doorstep mile'. As adults, it's often the thought of starting something new that paralyses us. We find excuses, we put it off, we make a cup of tea. Life goes on and the moment passes. It is this first small step that feels the hardest: a leap of faith from the known (safe, comfort, security) to the unknown (scary, unpredictable, risky). This can apply to most things: from clearing out the spare room, to starting a creative project, to beginning that new health regime, to joining a choir.

JUMP IN, THE WATER IS LOVELY!

In his talk at Do Lectures Wales in 2018, adventurer and blogger Alastair Humphreys talked about the importance of embracing the doorstep mile and encouraged us all to live more adventurously. He gave the example of when we go swimming in a river or a lake: we are initially apprehensive, we know the water will be cold, but once we get over the initial shock, we're splashing around and smiling, encouraging the people watching on the shoreline to get in too. This serves as a perfect analogy for your singing journey. Here the doorstep mile is walking through the door into a rehearsal or workshop for the first time, the journey from the known to the unknown. However, a world of positive, life-affirming singing awaits.

> **Stepping into the hall for that first rehearsal took every bit of strength I had, but by the time I left I knew I would keep coming. For those two hours, I felt the real joy of singing again, held by the warmth and friendship of the other members.**
>
> — Margaret, 86, retiree and great-grandmother

In this final section, I'll guide you through the steps to help you with your doorstep mile. This should give you the confidence and information you need to go out into the world and participate in group singing.

In the next chapter, I'll take you through a few simple exercises to help you reconnect with your singing voice, all of which you can do from the safety of your own home (or shower, or car!) There will be a focus on breath and posture plus a few song suggestions to get you going.

Then I'll guide you through the different options and choices when joining a singing group. There are many different types of choirs and I truly believe there is something out there for everyone: you might just need to take some time — and research — to find it.

And finally, at the back of the book I've included a Glossary in which I define a few basic singing terms that you might come across. OK, let's get you choir ready!

The human voice is the most perfect instrument of all.

Arvo Pärt

CHAPTER TEN
RECLAIM YOUR VOICE

The exercises that follow will help you unlock your voice and get you ready to sing. I do these in every session with my choirs and at my workshops.

Some vocal leaders call these type of exercises 'warm-ups' — I like to think of them more as preparation for mind, body, breath and voice. The principle of these is that singing is an extension of what we already do with our bodies and our voice (remember the Zimbabwean proverb: 'If you can walk, you can dance, if you can talk, you can sing').

The different stages of this are:

1. **Establish a good singing posture**

2. **Focus on your breath**

3. **Stretch and release tension**

4. **Explore your voice**

5. **Explore pitch: the five-note pattern**

6. **Start with a simple song**

ESTABLISH A GOOD SINGING POSTURE

The aim here is for a balanced resting position where you feel both relaxed and alert.

1. Stand with your feet a shoulder-width apart, with both feet flat on the ground.

2. Unlock your knees, so they feel soft and spongy.

3. Relax your shoulders; you might need to roll them a few times to do this.

4. Lift your head: imagine there is a thread pulling your head up (but keep your shoulders relaxed).

5. Let your arms fall loosely by your side. They should not be crossed, either behind your back or in front of you.

FOCUS ON YOUR BREATH

These exercises should help you focus and prepare for singing. They will also oxygenate the blood and make you feel more alert. Obviously, if you start to feel dizzy, sit down!

1. Take a deep breath in through your nose and breathe out through your mouth to a long 'sssh' sound. The outbreath should be longer than the inbreath. Repeat several times.

2. Breathe in through your nose for four slow counts, then breathe out through your mouth to a 'ssh' for *four* counts. Make sure your shoulders don't rise up as you breathe in. Repeat several times.

3. Breath in through your nose for four slow counts, then breathe out through your mouth to a 'ssh' for *eight*

counts. Make sure your shoulders don't rise up as you breathe in. Repeat several times.

4. Breathe in through your nose for four slow counts, then breathe out through your mouth to a 'ssh' for *twelve* counts. Make sure your shoulders don't rise up as you breathe in. Repeat several times.

5. Exhale all of the air out of your lungs, until there is nothing left. Don't actively breathe back in again, but let your lungs fill up naturally. This is known as 'letting the air drop in'.

STRETCH AND RELEASE TENSION

These exercises will help you stretch out and relax the shoulders, neck and face. Don't do these while driving!

1. Gently roll your shoulders, forwards and back, reducing any tension or stiffness.

2. Do some imaginary swimming! Slowly do forward strokes, then backstroke. This will open up your shoulders.

3. Keeping both feet on the ground, shake out your arms so they are loose, then your shoulders.

4. Give yourself a neck massage. Be aware of any tension and try to work this out gently.

5. Give yourself a face massage. Work the tips of your fingers around your temples, your jaw and your forehead.

EXPLORE YOUR VOICE

These exercises will help you connect with your voice and explore the sound you can make. Note: these exercises are not about singing, they are not about getting it right or wrong. These exercises use the speaking voice as a starting point for the singing voice.

1. Breathe in, hold for a few seconds, and do a long audible sigh. Repeat this several times, making the sound longer and going deeper each time.

2. Say 'ooh'. Now start the sound in the deep part of your voice and slide up and back down again. Aim to do this in one long continuous sound: it should sound as if you are impressed by something! Keep repeating the exercise, going higher each time. Then repeat on the sound 'eee'.

3. Say 'oh YES!' in a victorious way — as if your favourite team has scored a goal or a home run — going from the low part of your voice to the high part. You might want to do a fist-pump as you say 'YES!'

4. Say 'oh NOOOOOOO!' in a despairing way — as if your favourite team has just conceded a goal or home run — going from the low part of your voice to the high part and back again. You might want to put your head in your hands as you say 'NO!'

5. Try these different vocal sounds; be aware of how different they feel physically and where the sounds are produced: *hey, wow, OK, uh-oh, wee!* Now repeat and try to exaggerate the different vowel sounds. Be really playful, as if you are reading a story to a child.

EXPLORE PITCH: THE FIVE-NOTE PATTERN

Now we'll start to use a short, simple pattern using fixed notes (pitches).

1. Sing a five-note pattern using the notes 'doh-re-me-fa-so'. Start on a comfortable note in the low to middle part of your voice. You might need to adjust this a few times before it is comfortable. You could use numbers instead: one, two, three, four, five (or the same melodic pattern from the song 'Beauty and the Beast' that uses the lyrics 'ever just the same').

2. Sing the five-note pattern from 1 to 5 in one breath. Then sing from 1 to 5 then back to 1 in one breath, i.e. 1, 2, 3, 4, 5, 4, 3, 2, 1.

3. Use different vowel sounds to sing a five-note pattern on one sound, up and down: ooh, aah, ee, aaw, etc. Notice how the shape of your mouth is different for each one. Try to glide between the notes as smoothly as possible.

4. Now do the five-note pattern with short, separated sounds such as nah, la and ma. Try to be as accurate as possible and make sure each note is heard. Start slowly and gradually increase the speed of this.

5. To extend the range of your voice, try exercises 1 to 4 but with a slightly higher starting note. Only go as far as is comfortable: don't push too hard!

START WITH A SIMPLE SONG

Now have a go at singing a song. Keep it simple at this stage. A good place to start is with children's songs or folk songs, which tend to have a more restricted range of notes and have lots of repetition.

Here are some suggestions:

— **Twinkle, Twinkle, Little Star**

— **Frères Jacques**

— **Mary Had a Little Lamb**

— **Merrily We Roll Along**

— **Skip to My Lou**

— **For He's a Jolly Good Fellow**

— **Oh, When the Saints Go Marching In**

— **Swing Low, Sweet Chariot**

— **This Little Light of Mine**

Start small, start now.

Seth Godin

Put your spirit into that song.
Focus on the words that you are singing.
Get into the experience that you are
singing about and sing your heart out.

Stevie Wonder

CHAPTER ELEVEN
FIND YOUR
SINGING TRIBE

You're ready to go out into the world to sing. But where to start? There is a whole world of singing out there and this chapter will help you look at the options, so that by the end of it you might have a clearer idea of what you're looking for. And don't worry if you don't find the perfect group straight away: you can always try out a few groups before you find your singing tribe. But you'll know when you do. Here goes.

THE ONE-OFF WORKSHOP

If you are new to the world of group singing, the best place to start might be with a one-off workshop, rather than joining a weekly choir straight away. A workshop is when people come together to sing as a stand-alone event, which could last for anything from an hour to a whole day. Workshops often culminate in a final performance, maybe at the venue where you've been rehearsing, or it could be in the form of a 'flash mob' or it could be part of a bigger performance or concert. Sometimes the performance will be recorded and made available to you via email or social media after the event. For a good example of the workshop model, have a look at the 'Choir! Choir! Choir!' videos on YouTube.

Look out for workshops in your area or as part of local festivals. They may be led by local vocal leaders as a way of recruiting for a local choir. Or it could be with a touring artist, paired together with an evening performance. Workshops are often themed around a particular style or artist that may be of interest to you. There may also be one-off singing workshops offered at music festivals.

Examples of workshops I've led:

— 'Choir in a Day' where I taught four contrasting songs over the course of a day, leading to a final sing-through, recorded by participants on their phones (*40 people, 6 hours*)

— Creative Mornings in New York where I taught attendees 'Perfect Day' by Lou Reed in two-part harmony, filmed and available online (*200 people, 1 hour*)

— Co-leading the festival choir at The Good Life Experience in North Wales, where me and my friend Dom Stichbury led 2 x 90-minute rehearsals on consecutive days, leading to a final performance on the main stage at the festival (*60 people, 4 hours*)

— Co-leading a workshop with my performance group, The Fistful, where we taught 'Let's Dance' by David Bowie in an afternoon workshop, which the attendees then sang with us onstage that evening (*50 people, 2 hours*)

The beauty of workshops is that everyone is in the same boat: you are all learning together from scratch, so you won't feel at a disadvantage, as opposed to joining an established choir, for which you might have to do some catch-up. There is something very special about creating something quickly and in that moment — the rewards are almost instant! And to go back to Alastair Humphreys' analogy, it gives you a chance to dip your toes into the water before you fully plunge in. You'll undoubtedly feel that dopamine kick when the final performance is over.

It's at this point that you may feel like seeking a more regular singing group. But there's a lot of choice — use the following prompts to help you find something that will suit you.

WHAT TYPE OF CHOIR IS RIGHT FOR ME?

There are many different types of choir around: I believe that the right choir is out there somewhere for everyone. It might not be the first one you come across, it might not be the one nearest to where you live, but it's definitely worth doing some research. Look online — most choirs will have a website, which should give you a feel for what they do. But also look out for posters and flyers in your local community: often choirs are advertised on noticeboards in cafes and local shops. Hopefully the following questions will help you narrow down your search. Good luck!

WHAT TYPE OF MUSIC DO YOU WANT TO SING?

You might want to sing a particular genre — if so, then look for a group that specialises. This could include:

- Gospel
- Musical theatre
- Folk/traditional music
- Classical
- Light opera
- Contemporary rock/pop
- Barbershop
- Sacred music

If you like a broad range of music, you might want to look for a community choir that has a more varied repertoire across different styles.

A CAPPELLA, INSTRUMENTS OR BACKING TRACK?

'A cappella' means singing without any instruments. It comes from the Italian 'of the chapel', as the earliest form of notated vocal music was unaccompanied and sung in sacred buildings. A cappella is no longer the preserve of the church: you will find a cappella music in most singing styles, particularly in folk and traditional music. You might recognise contemporary pop a cappella from *Pitch Perfect* and *Glee*. Many choirs will perform a cappella exclusively and there are dedicated festivals around the world. It could be argued that a cappella is a genre in itself.

Both of my community choirs perform a cappella, for musical and practical reasons. Musically, there is something very satisfying about creating music purely from the human voice — using this to control the melodic, harmonic and rhythmic aspects of the sound. Practically, it means that you can sing anywhere — you always carry your voice with you! However, there are challenges that come with a cappella — you may feel more exposed without instrumental accompaniment and it can take longer to learn arrangements.

Many choirs are accompanied in rehearsal and performance by a piano or keyboard player. Alternatively, some are accompanied on guitar, particularly those that sing rock and pop styles. If you've always dreamed of singing with a live orchestra, many choral societies team up with a local orchestra for joint performances. Indeed, most professional orchestras have an amateur choir with whom they perform, although joining these usually requires an audition and the ability to read music.

Increasingly, choirs in rock, pop and music-theatre styles are using backing tracks in rehearsal and performance. A backing track is a pre-recorded song with the vocals taken out, like a karaoke track. This can work really well for groups who don't have access to an accompanist and those who want to have a full-sounding backing with drums, bass, guitar, keyboards, etc.

WHO DO YOU WANT TO SING WITH?

While some choirs are defined by the type of music they sing, some are defined by their demographic. Remember, choirs tend to be very sociable, so think about the environment you will feel most comfortable in. Some examples of demographic-based choirs include:

— All-male choirs
— All-female choirs
— Youth choirs
— Workplace choirs
— Choirs for older people
— LGBT+ choirs
— 'Sing for wellbeing' choirs
— 'Sing for health' choirs

HOW MANY PEOPLE DO YOU WANT TO SING WITH?

Think about the size of the group. Would you feel most comfortable in a large group, say around a hundred people, where your voice is a smaller part of a much bigger sound? Or would you prefer a smaller group, such as twenty people, where there will be fewer people on your voice part? There are pros and cons to both. It is easier to blend in (and hide if you want!) with a large group while still enjoying the powerful sound. You are more exposed in a smaller setting, which is definitely more challenging, but some might find this more rewarding.

HOW DO YOU WANT TO LEARN THE MATERIAL?

There is a preconception that in order to join a choir you have to be able to read music. However, this is not the case; reading music is just one approach to learning songs:

Musical notation: this is when you are given the sheet music for the songs you are singing to use in rehearsal and performance. The notation contains all the musical information you will need, such as melody, rhythm and dynamics, but this can be quite a challenge if you don't have experience of reading music. The words are printed underneath, so even if you are not a confident sight-reader you will be able to follow the words. Some choirs are very strict about music reading ability, some are a lot more relaxed. Always best to check if you're not sure!

Learning by ear: this is when you learn the music through listening and copying: the musical director will sing your part for you, which you then sing back in your section. Often you will be given a lyric sheet which you could annotate with lines, squiggles or whatever will help you remember your part.

Learning tracks: this is when you are given a CD or access to online materials so you can learn your individual part at home. You will be expected to know your part by the time you come to the rehearsal so that time can be spent getting the performance ready.

You will find that some choirs use one method exclusively, while some may use a variety of approaches. The one that's best for you will depend on your level of experience and the type of music that you want to sing. And, of course, what's available to you locally.

DO YOU WANT TO AUDITION?

I suspect that if you're an inexperienced singer, then the answer will be no. Many choirs these days are open-access, meaning that you don't have to do any kind of audition or singing test to join. This is the case with all of my choirs — taking the first step is difficult enough without having to sing solo in front of a stranger! However, if you have aspirations of singing solos with the group or want to join a performance-orientated group, you may have to audition.

HOW IMPORTANT ARE PERFORMANCES TO YOU?

Each choir will have a different expectation around performances. Think about what your priorities are here and what you can commit to. Most choirs usually have at least one or two performances each term that provides a focus for rehearsals. Some groups will have a busier schedule that all members are expected to commit to, while others will be more relaxed about attendance, especially those that are bigger in number. There are some choirs that don't perform at all, but simply enjoy singing together in rehearsals. While some people are happy to do this, I suspect that most choir members enjoy the thrill of a big performance (and enjoy that dopamine hit!)

DOES THE REHEARSAL VENUE WORK FOR YOU?

Think about where the group rehearses and if you'll feel comfortable in that environment. Also think about other practical factors, such as the distance you'll need to travel, proximity to public transport, parking, accessibility, times and duration.

Typical places where choirs rehearse are:

— Schools
— Churches
— Theatres
— Community halls

— Pubs
— Workplaces
— People's houses

HOW MUCH WILL IT COST?

This can vary. But generally, singing in a choir isn't an expensive hobby. A weekly rehearsal should be around the same price as a couple of coffees in a cafe (and the benefits will be felt for longer!) There are a number of payment models that choirs use, ranging from pay-as-you-go or paying for a block of rehearsals. There may be discount rates for those on lower incomes. Usually, a choir will offer a free taster session for prospective members so you can try before you buy. You can learn a lot from one rehearsal! There may be other extras such as hire of sheet music, purchase of learning CDs and buying the T-shirt.

WILL YOU GET ON WITH THE MUSICAL DIRECTOR?

The relationship between the musical director (MD) and the choir members is an important one. Indeed, the MD may be one of the main factors that determines whether you choose to stay in a choir. Every vocal leader has their own style and rapport with their singers, which might suit you or it might not. The only way to know is to go along to a rehearsal and find out. It is the job of the MD to make you feel supported, encouraged, challenged and inspired.

I don't sing because I'm happy;
I'm happy because I sing.

William James

EPILOGUE
NO REGRETS

I had a very powerful conversation with a singer at one of my residential singing weekends several years ago that has really stayed with me. The conversation took place on Llanddwyn Island, off Anglesey in North Wales, where, in the ruins of a sixteenth-century chapel, we gathered together to sing a gentle version of 'Amazing Grace' that we'd learned that weekend. It was a beautiful summer evening. After we'd sung, there had been a poignant silence for a few moments as we gathered our thoughts.

One of the singers came up to me and said, 'I've really loved it this weekend, thank you. I didn't tell you this when I arrived, but I haven't sung for over forty years. My wife died recently and I promised her that I would start singing again, because it brought me so much happiness when I was a boy. But I stopped singing because I was told by my teacher that I had a terrible voice. I believed him for all these years. I just wish I'd started sooner. I guess I just didn't get around to it.'

So, as we reach the end of this book, I hope this marks the beginning of the next part of your singing journey. I hope it has given you the insight and confidence to reclaim your voice, find your own singing tribe and experience the joy of group singing for yourself. And please don't leave it too late. As Mark Twain said:

Twenty years from now, you will be more disappointed by the things you didn't do than by the ones you did do. So throw off the bowlines. Sail away from the safe harbour. Catch the trade winds in your sails.

GLOSSARY

Here's a list of terms that I've either used in this book or you might come across when joining a choir. Note: some groups, particularly those using musical notation, may use further Italian musical terms, but these are not covered here.

A cappella
Singing without any instruments — just voices.

Chest voice
The low/medium part of your voice used in speaking. The sound is strong and full. It is called the chest voice because it feels like the resonance is in your chest.

Dynamics
The loudness of the music — the volume.

Harmony
When there are two or more different notes at the same time. Most choirs will sing in two-, three- or four-part harmony.

Head voice
The high part of your voice. The sound is lighter and clearer. It is called the head voice because it feels like the resonance is in your head.

Mixed choir
A choir for both male and female voices.

Musical director (MD)
The person responsible for leading the choir, often referred to as the conductor.

Pitch
How high or low a note is (not to be confused with dynamics).

Range
The distance between the highest and lowest note in a song.

Repertoire
The breadth of songs sung by a choir.

Soprano/Alto/Tenor/Bass
These refer to the different voice parts within a choir. They are listed in order of pitch, soprano being the highest and bass being the lowest. Soprano and alto tend be sung by female voices whereas tenor and bass are usually sung by male voices (although this isn't always the case; male altos and female tenors are quite common).

Unison
When everyone is singing the same tune, with no harmony.

RESOURCES

Here are the books, choirs, films and talks referenced through this book, plus a few others. For more on singing, community, wellbeing and creativity, please visit my blog: *everydaysinging.com*

Books

The World in Six Songs
— Daniel Levitin
The Little Book of Hygge
— Meik Wiking
Do Breathe
— Michael Townsend Williams
The Art of Gathering
— Priya Parker
The Top Five Regrets of the Dying
— Bronnie Ware
Flow
— Mihaly Csikszentmihalyi
This is a Voice
— Jeremy Fisher and Gillyanne Kayes

Films

The Chorus (2004)
Fisherman's Friends (2019)
Pitch Perfect (2012)
We Are Together (2006)

Choirs

Choir With No Name
Pub Choir
Koolulam
Choir! Choir! Choir!
Vokalkompagniet
The Spooky Men's Chorale
Wrexham One Love Choir
Ladysmith Black Mambazo

Talks

Flow: The Secret to Happiness
— Mihaly Csikszentmihalyi
  TED.com
How to Live Adventurously
— Alastair Humphreys
  thedolectures.com

ABOUT THE AUTHOR

James Sills is a musician and vocal leader with a passion for bringing people together to sing. He believes that singing together is a fundamental part of being human, fostering community, creativity and wellbeing. He leads a number of weekly open-access choirs, including workplace choirs in healthcare settings and a homeless people's choir. James also delivers workshops for groups and organisations across the UK, with a focus on inclusivity and confidence-building.

James leads the choir at The Good Life Experience, a festival in North Wales curated by Cerys Matthews, and is a member of the all-male a cappella troupe the Spooky Men's Chorale, with whom he has performed at festivals around the world. He is also a contributing songwriter and member of Rough Island Band, a contemporary folk quartet based in the Isles of Scilly.

His conviction in the transformative power of group singing has led James to give talks including Do Lectures (West Wales) and Creative Mornings (New York).

When he's not singing or making music, he can be found walking and trail running around the hills in North Wales where he lives with his family and vinyl collection.

You can connect with James via his website: *jamessillsmusic.co.uk* and blog: *everydaysinging.com* or via social media *@jsillsmusic*

THANKS

To everyone who has been part of my singing journey;
to anyone who has ever sung in my choirs or attended my
workshops. Thank you for giving your voice and giving
me the opportunity to do what I do. I literally couldn't do
it without you!

To my family, who have always supported me on my
various musical journeys, and for making me feel like
I am doing something important and worthwhile.

To those who have generously given me their time,
encouragement, instilled confidence, given me advice
and opportunities: Aunty Sheila, Sarah Whittaker,
Sense of Sound, Stephen Taberner, Charlie Gladstone,
Cerys Matthews, Dawn Foster, Tina Roth-Eisenberg.

To the Spooky Men's Chorale and the Rough Island
Band for life-enhancing music-making and friendship.

To Dom and Ian for invaluable feedback on the first
draft of the book; to all of those choir members who
shared their singing experiences with me to include in
this book.

To David, Clare and the whole team at Do Lectures
for creating something extraordinary and giving me
the opportunity to share my ideas (and songs) with the
attendees at Do Wales 2018.

To Miranda for asking me to write this book and for
your invaluable guidance. The Do Books series is something
I am incredibly proud to be part of.

And lastly, to my girls. For helping me be my best self.
This book is dedicated to you.

Index

Books in the series

Also available

Available in print and
digital formats from
bookshops, online
retailers or via our
website: **thedobook.co**

To hear about events and
forthcoming titles, you can
find us on social media
@dobookco, or subscribe
to our newsletter